It's Your Time

Time Management For Small Business and The Art Of Getting More Done

Peter Jewicz

[This Page Intentionally Left Blank]

All rights reserved. No part of this publication may be reproduced in any form or by any means, including scanning, photocopying, or otherwise without prior written permission of the copyright holder. Copyright 2019 Peter Jewicz and Total Web Connections LLC.

Published By Total Web Connections LLC

The 5 Steps To Taking Back Your Day 10

Know Yourself 13

Know What You Want 26

Prioritize and Plan 42

Concentration and Procrastination 75

Make It Routine & Building Habits 102

There's More To Effective Time Management 127

Master Your Inbox 128

My 10 Killer Productivity Tips 150

Your Turn 156

What's your schedule like?

Easy question right. But if you're anything like most business owners it's not as simple as that. Chances are if you're reading this book then your schedule is not a simple answer. Today I have to finish writing this book, update the website, don't forget about the social media, go over the analytics, set up the email list, make sure to finish coding the new feature, and that's all before noon!

If that sounds a bit like you then this book is for you. I wrote this book after struggling with time management and keeping to a schedule for years, so I know the struggle! As a millennial I'm addicted to my cell phone, constantly on YouTube, and always checking <Insert Hip Social Media Platform Here>. Obviously none of that really works for running a business or getting anything done really. Not only does it prevent business growth, but when you've spent the last last hour watching cat videos instead of doing the laundry your significant other isn't going to be happy. Not good.

But never fear! There's hope! If I could conquer my issues you can to! In this book I hope to dive into how to better manage your time. I'll go into what has personally worked for me, as well as additional techniques with which others have had success. By the end of this book I hope you give you the tools you need to understand yourself and your work style so you can better manage your time and schedule.

Everyone Is Different

It's true, ask any kindergarten teacher and they'll tell you that everyone is special in their own unique way. Jokes aside, it's true when it comes to what techniques are going to work for you.

That's unfortunately the truth, what works for me and keeps me organized might not work 100% for you. That's okay, though, and I've included lots of alternatives that will hopefully benefit you. This book isn't meant to be a 1:1 guide for everyone, but a base template to build upon. I'll talk about the key ideas, and how I implemented them, and then it's up to you to mold that to fit you and your work style.

The key to managing your time is to recognize the key pieces that lead to a hectic life. Each person is different in how they approach these keys, but the keys are all the same. If you can figure out what works for you then you'll be well on your way to wrangling up some extra time. And don't worry, I mention the keys here and we'll get to each one, that is what this book about is after all!

Time Ticks On

The important thing to realize is that time is our most valuable resource. We're put on this earth with a finite amount of it, and there's no way to make any more. The minutes, days, and years tick bye, un-caring and unstoppable.

While that's a bit bleak to think about it doesn't have to be. Take it heart and let it motivate you. Whenever I find myself staying or getting distracted I remind myself of the limited time I have to accomplish what I need to do.

That's not to say don't spend some time not worrying about it (we'll talk a bit about that later), but when you're in work mode make sure that you stay in work mode. We'll talk about motivation and what not a bit later, but it's important to keep time in perspective cause you're never getting more of it. Let that be part of your motivation.

The Power Of Choice

To round out this intro chapter I want to briefly touch on the power of choice. At the risk of sounding like a bad motivational speaker, you have the power to choose your life.

In context, that means you have the ability to make the decisions about how you spend your time. Simple right? But it's something to reiterate again and again.

Many people feel paralyzed by their schedule. I get it, I've been there. I know what it's like to have to have so much to do that it's hard to even know where to get started. Instead of giving up, I took charge, and started scheduling and prioritizing my work. It helped me get work done that needed to be done, and stop procrastinating and stalling.

It all started with a choice, a choice you now have by reading this book and acting on it. With that in mind, each further chapter has what I call "action items" at the end of it. These are the specific actions you can take right away, and should. Remember, you have the choice to do so or not, and only one of those is going to help you achieve your goals!

The 5 Steps To Taking Back Your Day

I'm a big fan of numbers and breaking things down into manageable steps, so to that end I've broken down this whole book into 5 key steps. If you take away one thing from this book it should be this next list of items. Now, obviously, each section is covered in more depth, but this is sort of like a 30,000 foot view of how I break down the process of planning and working efficiently. It is as follows:

1. Know Yourself - In order to plan efficiently you need to know what works for you, what doesn't work, and what keeps you motivated. Everyone is different in how they work, so play to your strengths.

2. Set Goals - Without goals what are you working towards? Good goals keep your on track.

3. Create a Schedule - Having your goals makes scheduling a breeze. Work on tasks that bring you there.

4. Master Working Efficiently - Beating back procrastination and learning to concentrate are keys to working effectively.

5. Make It Routine - Once you do something enough it becomes second nature. Make your scheduling and planning feel like that.

That's all there is to it. With these 5 simple steps you'll be the master of your schedule. Alright, maybe it won't be that easy, but it won't be as difficult as you might imagine. These 5 steps are the core ideas of this book, and exactly what I put into practice everyday to keep my schedule on track. I like to break it down like this as I think it makes things more manageable. Throughout the rest of the book I hope to help you implement them all into your daily life, and build a killer routine that makes it all second nature.

I already touched on this, but at the end of each section I also include what I'm creatively calling "action items". These are the practical steps that put into the an actual task to complete based on the previous chapter. If you really want to get the most out of this book then take this part seriously. Actually take the time to implement these, and don't just say "I'll get around to it". I mention them again here to hopefully show how important they are. If all you do is read this book then you'll get nothing out of it. Taking the time to actually put into action the ideas in this book if you want to see results.

With all that in mind, I'm not a big fan of long winded intros, so let's jump right into the meat of it and learn about some time management!

Know Yourself

Wait a second, I thought we were going to start talking about time management? In due time, but first there's a couple of things you need to understand about yourself. You see, in order to really make in change in yourself, you need to understand yourself. Make sense?

So before we jump into the actual strategies, let's take a minute to reflect on ourselves. I promise it won't take long, but it is just as important as any other step so take it seriously.

Track Your Time

While not groundbreaking in anyway, tracking your time is essential to wrangling in your time problems. It's easy to do, but super effective and can reveal a lot about yourself.

The point of time tracking is to figure out exactly how you spend your day and exactly how much time various things take. It's easy to say thing X takes 1/2 hour, but without clear data how do you know? It could take a full hour and you're just underestimating; or on the flip side could take 15 minutes and the rest is filled with scrolling through Facebook.

The point is to help you later when you're looking to schedule and prioritize tasks. If you don't have a decent idea of how long something takes then it's difficult to create a schedule around it. Trust me on that, there's nothing worse than scheduling a bunch of tasks on Monday only to still be working on them on Thursday when you underestimated how long they would take.

It's also important to understanding where you're wasting

time. If you're working for 3 hours, but noticing that half of that is on YouTube you immediately have something to work on. The act of tracking can also work as a deterrent too. It can be tiresome to track every little activity, and knowing you'll have to account for that 5 minutes on Facebook can make it less likely you'll do so.

Time tracking is also a skill that develops over time. I always say to track your time strictly for at least a month, but after that it's okay to relax a little bit on it if your intuition is taking over.

As you do it more, you'll get better an innately knowing how long things are going to take. This is especially true with things you do often as you'll naturally track them multiple times. Over time, you can cut back on how strictly you track time, while still reaping the benefits of knowing how to properly schedule your day.

So now that we have the theory out of the way, how do you actually track your time? You have a couple of good options. Side note; this is the first instance where different people will gravitate towards different things. Depending on what you like, you might find some of these options more effective than others. Give each of them a try, and stick with what feels more natural to you.

Pen & Paper

The old fashion way of doing things, but great for those who like having a physical copy of things. Keeping a log of hours with simply pen and paper is perfectly fine, and you don't need to learn anything new to do it. Make sure you're strict about it though, keep your log always in reach so you're never tempted to slack.

Mobile Apps

My personal favorite option is a mobile app. Having it on my phone means my time is always on me, and I can start it up easily. Keep in mind though, your phone is a big distraction, so I'll often start the timer, and then leave the phone in other room or just out reach while I work. This also encourages me not to switch tasks as the act of getting my phone is an inconvenience in itself.

Online Software

Similar to mobile apps, there are tons of desktop and online programs for your computer that track time. Many of these also have a mobile app, so you can get the best of both worlds!

Overall, just make sure you find a good way to track your time and you stick to it. The data it gives you will help you out immensely in the long run. I can't stress enough how important it is to be strict here. 5 minutes of social media might not seem worth it to track, but when you do that 20 times a day it really adds up. It can be eye opening how much time you waste on seemingly quick distractions, and that's what this part is all about.

Know Your Motivation

Let's face it, none of want to work just for the sake of it. Sure there might be some workaholics out there always grinding away, but for the rest of us it's important to be working towards something. It's good to have motivation and to frequently remind yourself of that motivation.

Maybe you want a new car, maybe a house, or maybe you just want to provide for your family. Whatever the reason it always helps to have small reminders near your workstation. Many people choose to have pictures or some sort of other small imagery. Maybe make your desktop background that new Maserati you're looking to get?

Whatever it is be loud and proud about it and let it help drive your work. It's okay to be a bit vain at times if it helps you muscle through otherwise unproductive periods. Whenever you think about logging into Facebook or watching another Youtube video think about what you're working towards; trust me it helps!

Know Your Weaknesses

I know I know it's hard to analyze yourself, but it seriously helps! If you don't know where your weaknesses are then how can you expect to make improvements on them?

This is where time tracking can really come in handy as it can help you understand how you spend your day. If you think you're slamming down 16 hour days but in reality are spending half of that goofing around then that's a problem.

The key then is to be honest with yourself and figure out how to correct the problem. Later on in this book we go over some procrastination and concentration tips, and these can help if that's the root of the problems.

This will become more important when we talk about procrastination as that's a big problem for most, so we'll talk about it more there. Keep this in mind though through the rest of the book as the first step to fixing any problems is to identify them and admit they are there.

Know Your Sweet Spot

If you're anything like me you have that sweet spot during the day when you get the most work done. Some people love the mornings and can jump right into things quickly. Others might be night owls, and get the most done when everyone else is asleep.

The key is to not fight against this, but play into it and make it work for you. If you're a night owl, then schedule your most important tasks at night and not in the morning. Part of being a productive business owner is doing what works for you, and understanding the times where you get stuff done. Don't try to force yourself to wake up early just because some "expert" said that's good to do if you're seeing results on your own schedule.

You'll also want to treat this time preciously and set yourself up for success. In a later chapter we talk about beating procrastinating, and you'll want to make sure you use those tips to the fullest during this time.

That all said, you still have to work your schedule around your clients or other obligations. Only being available to take calls after 9pm is going to not work in most cases, so still think about your schedules realistically.

Make a Daily Win List

It's not all doom and gloom, sometimes it pays to step back and reflect on a job well done. At the end of each day take 5 minutes out and reflect on the progress for the day.

This helps keeps things in perspective, and you'll often be surprised at how much you actually get done! It's also a good way to look back on days when maybe you didn't get as much done as you'd hoped to, and make plans to dive into it tomorrow. I always spend a few minutes at the end of the workday reflecting on the day. It's not only a good way take stock of my progress, but also helps set me up for tomorrow's work.

It's also a good way to stay motivated throughout the day. Competing with yourself to get more done by the end of the day is a good way to push through those slow periods and stay on track. A lot of people like to "gamify" their work, this is kind of like that; you're competing against yourself.

Action Items

You've reached the end of the first section and are now at what I'm calling your action items. While reading through the theory is great, sometimes it can be hard to apply to your day to day life.

Never fear though! I'm here to get your back! At the end of each chapter you'll get a brief list of things you can start doing today to apply the lessons you learned throughout the chapter. I highly recommend you do if you want to get the most out of this book. Many people will read it, and say something like, "Oh that's nice, maybe I'll start doing that". But they never do, and consequently never see results.

Don't end up like that. Read over these action points and resolve to start doing them today. Not tomorrow, not next week, but not yesterday either; today. Your future self will thank you for it!

1. Start Tracking your time - Grab a piece of paper, an app, or whatever and start tracking what you do for at least the next two weeks. Track both work tasks as well as other things you do during your work time. This will help you make schedules later, and also show you how much time you're potentially wasting.

2. Find Something To Motivate You - Figure out what you're working towards and bring something that reminds you of it to your workstation. Maybe you want a new car or a bigger house, or maybe just to provide for your family. Whatever it is make it prominent and let it serve to motivate you everyday. This isn't necessarily a work goal (we'll get to that later), but something that personal motivates you to work harder.

3. Figure Out Where You Waste Time - Using the tracking above or your intuition figure out where you waste the most time and stop yourself every time you find yourself about to. Also, really focus on the concentration/procrastination chapter below and let that help you fight your time wasters.

4. Reflect Daily - Take a few minutes to reflect at the end of the day on your progress. Then resolve to do better the next day! Use this as an opportunity to acknowledge both your wins, as well as areas where you can improve. Critical reflection, both positive and negative, is a good way to stay motivated and improve yourself.

Know What You Want

Before we jump into planning and scheduling it's important to take a step back and figure out exactly what you're working towards. This shifts gears a bit from above, it's not just your personal motivation, but what your business is trying to achieve. A new car is great to keep you motivated, but landing 10 new clients this month is more in line with the business's needs. This section will focus on the later, and help you set business goals to keep your on track.

The reason having clear goals is so important is that it's impossible to prioritize without them. If you don't know what the end goal is there's no good way to measure how important any particular task is, which in turn makes create schedules difficult. This then leads you to aimlessly wander, with no direction, randomly picking work. I was stuck here, and it wasn't until I started setting smart goals to work towards that I really hit my stride.

What we want is to figure out which tasks are most important to achieving your businesses goals. This allows you to focus your time on the most important tasks and be more productive overall.

As we'll get into later, being able to measure a tasks worth against a goal is essential to wrangling in your time. With that in mind, let's get goal setting so we can move onto the really juicy meat of this book.

SMART Goals

Something I totally came up with on my own is SMART goals. Okay, I didn't, but that doesn't make them any less important!

SMART is an acronym that defines a specific way to create and set goals. This helps make them more directed, which makes them easier to track and ultimately achieve. Let's take a quick look at what each letter means and what SMART goals look like, and how they work together.

S: Specific - Your goals should be clear, specific, and easy to understand. Something like "I want my businesses to make more money" is not really a good goal because it's very ambiguous. There's not a good way to tell whether you've hit that goal or not. Does a penny increase count, or does it need to be more?

"I want to raise profits by brining in 10 new clients" on the other hand is much better. It's specific in both it's end goal as well as the key step needed to achieve it. A good way to write specific goals is to answer the 5 w's, who, what, when, where, and why. The goal you set should have a very clear criteria for complete or not.

M: Measurable - Good goals are also measurable in the sense that you can gauge progress on them. This is also important for motivation as seeing yourself inch closer to your goal is simply a great feeling. Taking the example above, "Make More Money" is not a good goal as while you can measure it there is no sense of progress and no clear completion criteria. Something like "Make $10,000" is much better as you can easily check your progress against the goal, and know exactly when it's achieved.

A: Achievable - A good goal is also realistic, you actually have to be able to hit it. This is a bit tricky as what might be unrealistic for one businesses or person might not be for another. Put some thought into this one, and come up with something that both pushes you, but is achievable. You don't want something too easy or too hard. Brining in 1,000,000 new clients seems a bit absurd, but brining in 100 might be much more realistic.

Don't make them too easy either! A goal that you blow right past does little motivate you once you achieve it. Pick something that hurts a little to achieve, but not too much as to make it seem impossible. There should always be some friction in achieving your goals, that's what drives us to improve.

R: Relevant - Good goals are also directly related to your business. This might seem like a no-brainer, but you'd be surprised how many people spend hours working on things that aren't going to help grow. Pick things that directly impacts the bottom line of your business, profits, customers, clients, ect; all good choices just to name a few.

T: Time bound - Lastly, goals need to be capped by some deadline. You don't want to have a goal go on to infinity, as then there is no sense of urgency attached to it. This also goes back to achievable; your timeline directly influences what is achievable. Giving yourself a cap of 6 months or a year is generally a good place to start, but it's okay to have multiple goals running that span larger or short time periods. I like to create yearly goals, then break them down into mini-goals for each month. This helps make them more manageable, while still working towards my long term plans.

Now that we've got all that down let's put it all together to come up with a SMART goal. Let's take the first bad example:

"I want my business to make more money"

It's a bad goal for a couple of reasons. It's not specific, you can't measure it, it has no way to measure how achievable , and it has no timeline. The only thing you might argue is good about it is that it's relevant, but that's only because it mentions money which most businesses want.

Now let's reword it the SMART way.

"I want to bring in 10 new clients to my business to increase our profits, and I want to do so within the next 6 months"

Well would you look at that, that's one fine looking goal. It's now specific in that it talks about exactly what it is, you can easily measure it, on the surface it looks achievable, it's definitely relevant, and has a clear timeline.

Setting goals in this manner helps to make sure they're doing the most to benefit you. Having goals is also shown to help increase productivity by giving you something to work for. If you've ever felt like you're just kind spinning your wheels then setting goals is a great way to keep you focused and on track.

Don't you feel smarter already?

Challenging But Realistic

The "A" in SMART is achievable, and I want to take a second to look a bit deeper in that. Setting achievable goals can be a bit challenging.

The mantra I live by is "Challenging but Realistic", you want goals that push you just a bit. My rule of thumb is to take what I see as a doable goal, and then stretch it by 15-20%.

The logic is that even if I miss this goal I still hopefully achieve more than I would have initially set. That extra bit helps motivate me, and keeps me honest when I'm working. Never settle for less than your best, and don't fall into the trap of setting goals that are too easy and losing steam once you hit them.

Long Term and Short Term

Personally, I'm a big fan of having a set of both long term goals, as well as a set of shorter term goals. My long term goals might span an entire year or longer. On the flip side, my short term goals are usually month to month or sometimes even shorter. As I mentioned earlier, I use my longer goals to set my short term goals. If I have a one year goal, I might break it up into 12 smaller goals that I look to complete each month.

This gives me a good range of items to achieve and work towards, while providing that warm fuzzy feeling of regularly meeting my goals each month. Sometimes it can be a bit hard to stay motivated for something 10 months away, so it can help to have a tangible goal with a deadline in only two weeks.

For example my long term goal might be to increase profits 20% on the year, while a short one might be to bring in 4 new clients by months end. This might not work for everyone, but I'm a huge fan of splitting it up like this.

It also makes staying on track easier. In most cases, the

monthly goals will directly impact the yearly goals. In the above example, bringing in new client is certainly going to help me increase profits overall. Even better is if I know roughly how much each client is worth, and 4 new clients per month gets me to that 20% I'm shooting for. In this way, you can easily see if you're on track or not, and can adjust well before the year long deadline.

If you don't want to create separate monthly goals you can also simply break down your yearly goal into chunks and look to hit those each month. In the above example if I calculate I'll need 48 new clients to reach my sales goals then breaking that down to 4 each month both helps me stay on track as well as make the task at hand seem more manageable. 48 clients might seem impossible, but getting 4 this month seems a lot more doable!

Remind Yourself Of Your Goals

You're also going to want to regularly evaluate your goals as time goes by. You want to know whether you're on track to hit your goals, or if you're way off base and need to pivot.

Here's a secret, it's okay to change your goals. Really it is! As your business and work evolves so will your goals. Maybe you set your goals a bit too lofty, or perhaps a bit too easy, that's okay. This isn't an exact science and you're bound to need to re-evaluate at some point.

Don't see that as a sign of failure but as a sign of growth and progress. Like any skill, the more you do it the better you'll get and doing it, and the more realistic, achievable, and beneficial your goal setting will become. In the meantime, there's nothing wrong with adjusting your goals on the fly to match reality.

Just don't be the person to adjust their goals out of laziness. If you're adjusting your goals to avoid having to work a bit harder then shame on you! Only adjust a goal if you've made a mistake on the difficulty of achieving it.

Keep Track Of Your Progress

With any goal, you want to keep a close watch on your progress to make sure things are moving along at the correct pace. The whole point of having goals is to make sure that you're hitting them, and there's no way to know that without tracking them!

The method of tracking is going to differ from person to person and even on a per goal basis in some cases. For many, a simple spreadsheet or word doc with the goals key milestones is enough. I personally have a google doc folder setup for each of my projects, and then setup a file there where I can track the various goals for each one. I can then record my progress, and even go back and see past progress from previous goals. This lets me evaluate things like how often I hit my goals, which in turn can help me plan better in the future.

I also like the method of writing goals down on a big whiteboard in my office. There I have a list of my current goals for the month, and a small note on the progress. This makes sure I'm always aware of where I'm at progress wise, and forces me to acknowledge my goals each and every day. I like to use my monthly goals here as it forces me to update the board more often and I enjoy the feedback of writing on my white board.

Outside of that, there's tons of apps and other ways to record and track your goals. Apps are a great way to track as they can often spit out reports and metrics to see how often you hit goals long term. This can help with future planning to ensure you are setting realistic goals.

In the end though, it doesn't matter how you do it, but make sure you are. Use what works best for you, it will likely be similar to how you track time.

Continually Revaluate

Building off the last point, now that you're keeping track of your goals, make sure to revisit and reevaluate. I like to do this in two ways.

One is to set a specific amount of time where I go back and

reevaluate my goals. Every couple of months I take some time out to check on my goals, usually at the end of the quarter. I try to see that I'm not only working towards my goals, but that the metrics I set are still relevant to my business. For example, maybe I realized that I was neglecting the power of return customers, and so I modify my goals to focus more on repeat business than acquiring new clients.

The other is to do so after business changes in some significant way. Maybe I landed a big client, or lost a big client, and that significantly alters what I'm able to do. There's no use in waiting months; I like to step up and revaluate right away. This can help keep my goals in that lofty but reachable range, which is important to keep me working at my best. It also helps keep things relevant to your businesses as a big change like mentioned above can completely change what you can do.

Drawing off the example above, maybe your goal was to increase profit 10% on the year, but you land a client in February that alone gives you an 8% boost. Instead of patting yourself on the back and slacking the rest of the year take this as an opportunity to re-evaluate your goals. Now, instead of going for 10% you might decide to aim a bit higher and shoot for 20%.

Whatever you decide, the important thing is to regularly reevaluate your progress, and make sure you're still on track. As mentioned above, it's okay if things change and you need to readjust your goals. Setting goals to begin with is tricky, and with how fast things can change in business it's impossible to know what next week can bring.

Action Points

Now that you've got some idea about setting goals let's go through and get some written down. There's no need to be super thorough at this point, just spend a little time and come up with a handful of key metrics and milestones for your business. You can always (and should) come back later and readjust, remove, or add to the list.

1. **Set a short term goal**. Something you want to get done in the next month or two. It should be something that pushes you, but is still doable. If you're having trouble here, come up with a long term goals first and then set a reasonable chunk of that to do in the next month.

2. **Set a long term goal**. Think of something you want to do this year and write it down. This could be a number of clients, a revenue goal, or something else. Once again, this should be difficult, but not un-doable. Aim to set something too high rather than too low.

3. Start tracking your goals. Figure out how you want to, and start updating progress towards your goals on a weekly basis. Take a few minutes and record how much closer you made it this week or month. If you're not sure how to start, go grab a notebook and just record it there for now. Low tech, but it works!

4. Set a reminder to revaluate your goals. On your phone or calendar, set a reminder a month from now to revaluate your goals. Take an honest look at your progress, and adjust if needed. Then, do it again the month after!

Prioritize and Plan

Now, we're finally getting to some of the real meat of this book. If you're like me, you've struggled with the actual planning and prioritization of tasks, and that's a big problem. Without proper planning it's difficult to know what you can get done, and makes it impossible to estimate when projects will be complete. If you've had problems before then this is the section for you. By the end you'll have the skills to become a pro planner.

Proper planning is not easy though, it's difficult to know how much time to allot to a task, and even more difficult to account for unexpected delays. We've all been there, we thought something would be quick and easy, but ends up consuming an entire day. Those tasks stink, and it's impossible to account for them all, but with proper planning we can minimize their effect, and be more productive overall.

The big drag here is there is no silver bullet, or quick easy way to do this. Each person is likely to plan in a different way, and that's okay. I personally love to assign everything on a big calendar, and then have my weekly tasks in front of me. This works for me, but might not for everyone. Some people like to write everything down by hand in planners, while others are fine using apps that sync across devices. It doesn't matter what your preference is, but find something that works for you and stick to it.

During this chapter, we're going to start with some general guidelines and ideas about scheduling, and then dive into some techniques for actually planning. I'll also share with you the steps I take to build my own schedule, which will hopefully inspire and help you to create your own. Having these guidelines in mind will help you make smarter decisions when it comes to figuring out how to schedule tasks.

Figure Out How Long Things Take

Before we get into actually scheduling it's important to start getting a feel for how long things take you to do. Without these numbers it's difficult to correctly gauge how long a task takes you and how much you can handle in a day. Part of the big problem of not having timings is either scheduling too much or too little in a day. Once you start getting a feel for timing you'll have much more accurate schedules.

The problem here is that the only good way to really get a feel for this is with experience. If you're relatively new to whatever it is you're doing it can be difficult to make accurate estimates. Experience is one of the only true way to get better at estimates, and that takes time.

That's why we started tracking time though right? It's critical that you start doing so if you haven't already, as having the data will really help making your schedules easier in the beginning. Being able to look at a similar task that took 2 hours will help you plan that next task. As you get more experience your intuition is likely to take over and be fairly accurate, but until you get to that point having numbers to help you is invaluable.

I can't stress enough how important this is. A schedule that is wildly off in time estimates is almost as useless as just not having one. If you're not already tracking time at this point then get to it.

One Place To Write It Down

A big thing I preach about schedules is to pick one method to record them and stick to it. It doesn't matter how you do it, just make sure you are staying consistent and not being all wishy washy and switching it up every week.

There's a certain power that actually writing something down has, and it makes it so much more likely you'll actually do it. Putting your commitment out into the world makes it far more likely you'll do it than just keeping those ideas in your head. There's some science behind it if you want to look it up, but for now just take my word for it.

Now, when I say "writing it down" I don't necessarily mean with a pen and paper, although that is an option. I mean just finding a way to commit your thoughts into the world. There are a ton of good apps and software out there that help with project planning and scheduling, and if that's something that works for you then it's absolutely fine to use them. For those that like the physically of pen and paper that's fine too. A nice planner is always a good choice as well.

The point is that it doesn't matter what you use to plan and prioritize your work, but you need to find something that works for you and stick to it. Choose one option and stick to it for a few weeks to see how you like it, and then evaluate how you can improve.

One of the biggest mistakes you can make is to constantly be switching how you plan your time. So many people will start with one system, use it for a few days, and then switch to another. In the end, they spend so much time learning and implementing a new system that they end up wasting more time than they gain. If you're going to try a new way of scheduling, give it a fair shake and spend some serious time with it before making any changes. You really want to be sure that the time you open on a new system is justified.

Worst Task First and The Art of 80/20

Okay, that title is a bit weird, but bare with me. Each of these is a take on task prioritization, and are actually important things to keep in mind. Implementing both of these rules into my work has help me become significantly more productive.

The worst task first principle means that if you start your day with your worst task the day only goes up from there. In business terms, that means getting your most unpleasant or difficult task done first. This not only provides momentum, but is just a great way to keep focused on what's important. If you've taken care of the least pleasant task right away, then you can take comfort that the rest of your day will be easier or more enjoyable.

The 80/20 principle is the idea that 80% of your results coming from only 20% of your tasks. This means that a large portion of your tasks are way less important and don't contribute as much as only a small minority do.

The basic idea here are that not all tasks are created equal. There are simple things you need to do that are more important than others. This is important for maximum productivity as you want to make sure you're focusing on what really matters. To that end, never be afraid to step back and evaluate your work. If there's something you're doing that's not bringing in the results you want then find a way to cheaply outsource or automate it. That way you can be freed up to do the tasks that matter.

Think about it kind of like the CEO compared to a regular employee. The CEO get's paid the big bucks to make the high level, super important decisions. The CEO's decisions are those 20% that account for the majority of growth (or failure). That's not to say the normal employees job is not important, it's essential, but it doesn't have the overarching effect that the CEO has. A CEO's decision can make or break a company, their choices have a large effect on the overall health of the company.

Always look to keep the important stuff for you, and give away as much as you can of the other 80%. The more you can offload to other, the more time you'll have for the really important stuff. You're the metaphorical (or literal) CEO of your company, so try to back your day with work that matters and only you can do.

This also ties back in with "Finding Your Sweet Spot" I mentioned before. Once you start figuring out a hierarchy for your tasks, then you can start placing them during your most productive time. Focusing on those 20% of most important tasks during your sweet spot is a no brainer.

The Myth Of Multi-Tasking

One of the big productivity myths of our time is that of multitasking. People who claim to be "multitaskers" are the type of people who say they can scroll through social media, while talking on the phone, while jotting down notes. While some of us might feel this is possible the science is not on our side and trying to multitask is generally less efficient. Maybe some truly can do it, but most of us can't.

The truth is that our brains are not very good at handling more than one thing at a time. When you try the brain has to "switch" from one process to the other. This "switch" isn't seamless, and ends up taking time to fully happen.

This makes it quite inefficient to try and do multiple things at once. The only times where this doesn't play is when one of the activities is so thoroughly mastered it's almost second nature. An expert musician might be able to play their instrument while holding a conversation, but they are the exception and not the rule and they certainly didn't start with that skill.
The point is that when you're looking to create your schedule make sure your time is spent to focus on a a single task or set of related tasks. Group like tasks together helps cut down on the time your braining is "switching". This helps you stay focused and productive, and cuts down on the effect distractions have on you. We'll talk about this idea a bit more when we look at batching, but for now try to give each task it's own dedicated time.

Creating Your Schedule

Now that we've got some of the general ideas out of the way let's take a more in depth look at actually creating a schedule. I'll start by giving you an example of what I do to create my daily/weekly/monthly schedules, so you can see one way it's done.

I also want to stress that it is only one way to do it, how I like my schedule might seem awful to you, and that's perfectly okay. Everybody has their own style and as much as this book is a guide to better time management I also want it to encourage you to discover your own unique style. Treat this section as almost like a template, and then use it to build your own style.

So without further ado, let's build a schedule!

Figure Out Your Planning Style

As I mentioned before figuring out your own style is important to make planning and scheduling as easy as possible. To that effect I want to talk a bit about how I build my own schedule. While it might not work 100% for you, the thought is it might give your ideas on how you can make your own.

I've broken the way I make my schedule into a few key points to make it easier to digest. Each of these points plays an important role in the overall process, so let's jump right in.

1. Start With Your Goals

The first thing I do is always keep my end goals in mind and plan around that. I generally have yearly goals, which then allow me to reverse engineer what I need to do each month. For example, if my goal is to make $12,000 for a year then that's roughly $1,000 per month. Now it's not as cut and dry as that, you should ideally be improving each month, but you get the idea. If you've made other monthly goals already then you can use these too.

Using these monthly/weekly goals I'm then able to generate the tasks I need to complete. Generally, I have all the tasks I need to complete for a project generated at the start of the project, but if not I can do so here. I'll spend a good amount of time thinking about all the tasks I need to complete for a project and jot them down. At this point I now have a list of all the tasks I need for a particular project, as well as the goals I'm looking to achieve.

With this, I can then create plans by the week and then by day in order to reach my goal for the month. This lets me focus on the tasks that are directly impactful for achieving my goals. This is also why good goal setting is extremely important or it would be much more difficult to schedule my tasks each day.

The key idea here is that all your tasks should be working towards the goals you've set. This also helps you determine which tasks are important later on.

2. Identify Working Time

The next step is to figure out how much time you actually have to work. This is especially important if you're a part time owner and have a full time day job as your time will be at an absolute premium; or if you have other obligations like being a parent that cuts into your working hours.

Be honest with yourself here, if you only have 20 hours a week then only budget that. Don't assume you'll be a superhero and tack on extra. If you do, great, you'll be ahead of the game, but if you don't you won't throw off your whole schedule. There's no use in creating a schedule that's going to be impossible for you to stick to.

This is a huge problem, and one that I actually suffered from for quite some time. I would create elaborate plans of the work I was going to do; work that would at least take a full 40 hours. Then I would get home from my day job, and that 6 hour work session I planned would degrade into only 2-3. This really throws off your schedule, and it is honestly a bit demotivating. Be honest with yourself and you'll be better at estimating, and you won't end up with the crushing task of having to replan half a week of work every couple of days.

Another important step I take is to take your estimate and knock off around 10% to account for wasted time, delays, and other instances of inefficient use of time. If I had 20 hours to work each week, then I might only actually schedule about 18 hours of work. This is important as almost no one is 100% efficient, and doing this will make your estimates more accurate.

At this point, you should look to have a handful of tasks picked out at that match up with how much time you have to work. These tasks should also directly line up with your goals above, which is how I was able to create them in the first place.

This is also a great place to evaluate how realistic your goals are. If everything lines up, then great! However, if you notice that you don't have enough working hours to hit your goals that's a potential red flag. It doesn't mean you should change your goals (as difficult goals are often motivating), but it's certainly something to keep an eye on. You may need to lessen the goal later, or cut down to focus on less if you have multiple goals/projects at once.

If you're in a boat where you have more tasks than you can handle in a week then the next section is doubly important for you.

3. Prioritize Tasks

As we mentioned before not all tasks are created equal. You want to spend some time really looking at your tasks and figuring out what is most important. This is also a good place to prune down if you have too many tasks. By focusing on what's important you ultimately get more done as you spend less time on meaningless tasks.

In most cases, you're going to have more on your plate than you can handle. This is especially the case if you have multiple ongoing projects. You need to be able to prune your task list; going off your goals and the task importance is the best way to do this.

This can be really hard to do, as in many cases a lot of tasks can see like they're all important to your bottom line. The truth is though, in most cases there are some that are slightly more important than others. It's your job to understand your business and find out what is the key to its success. You also likely have some tasks that depend on others, which makes it easy to know which order to do them in.

With that said, in most cases you're going to want to focus on your revenue generating tasks. If something is brining in new clients/customers and paying the bills it's usually pretty important. This might also be outreach to existing or past clients/customers; whatever is brining in those dollars.

Another good candidate is tasks that fit into your long term goals, and might be profitable in the future. For example, social media might not be great for your now, but your goal is to spend the next year building a following. This has future potential to reward dividend, and depending on your business might also qualify it as an important task.

A lot of this is making estimates and choosing the best option. It's hard to know how effective a particular task might be compared to another, but that's something you need to figure out as you go along. Part of being a successful business owner is making those tough decisions with limited information. That's somewhat of a non-answer, but truly what matters to your businesses is unique and something you should work to determine.

In this process you don't necessarily want to remove tasks from your to-do list, but just reorder them in terms of importance. I like to keep a backlog of less important tasks that I can do later on, or fill holes in my schedule with.

4. Estimate Work

Now that you've got and idea of how much time you have to commit, and your tasks prioritized, it's time to actually fill that with work. This is why it's so important to get a feel for how long things actually take (AKA track it), so that you can properly fill out your time.

With good estimates, it's easy to be able to fill your allotted time. Simply match your allotted scheduled time with your tasks going from most important first.

An important note on why this section here is this is an iterative process. You might find that after the first pass you have a few larger tasks that don't necessarily fit into your schedule, and that's okay. It's perfectly okay to push those tasks until next week and go back and find some that fit your remaining schedule. This makes this process not really a steps 1-4 like it's written, but an interchangeable process that's fluid.

For actually making my final schedule I like to work backwards, and assign tasks for roughly a month in order to get to my goal. If I end up with extra time then I pull in some of the less important or next months tasks. If I don't have enough, then I can realize very quickly my goals may be too lofty. It's a very trickling effect as you can quickly see from the very first month how much extra work you'll have to put in.

A note on estimating, whenever I work out the time for a task I always tack on an extra 10%. Even though I've been a developer for years, I still make mistakes and miscalculations, so having that bit of breathing room ensures I'll usually have time to spare. This is likely different for other industries where tasks might be a bit more consistent, but it's not a bad practice to get into.

At this point you should have full schedule, congratulations! The important thing here is to get into the habit of doing this often, and eventually it will just become second nature and you won't even think about doing it.

Daily/Week/Month

Personally, I like to create a schedule for my days, my week, and my month. This might seem like a bit overkill for some, but I personally thrive on having a plan. I treat it almost like a mini game each day and there's a good sense of pride when you check off a long list of to-dos. This in turn builds momentum, and is a great psychological boost.

Basically, I do exactly as I said in the section above, I simply go backwards each month to figure out what I need to achieve that goal. I then estimate the time it takes to do all that work, and spread it across the month. I do a rough draft each month, and then each week go back and give it a bit more detail, adjusting if needed.

If you're new to creating your schedule I highly recommend you at least start with this type of planning. While it's not for everyone, it's hard to know until you actually try it, and it only takes a few minutes each day. Give it the fair shake I mentioned earlier, and after a few weeks if you hate it try something new. I know very successful people who only come up with monthly plans and pick from that, so there's more than one effective way to do this.

What About By The Hour?

While I personally don't do this, some people thrive by having their entire day planned out and scheduled, so I'll mention it here. If you're this type of person then there's nothing wrong with this.

In this method, you take the day a step further and block out your time down to the hour or even minute on what you should be working on. This is especially helpful for those who have a strong handle on how long tasks take, as well as those who have a lot of meetings. It's also a great way to stay focused as saying you'll be working on graphics from 1-3 makes it that much more likely you actually will. There's a power to having something in writing!

The big downside here, and why I tend to shy away from being this granular, is when you're working with difficult to predict tasks. If you're planned down to the minute, then even a 30 minute overage can mean problems. This is why I generally think of my day in chunks as opposed to hours.

For example, I might group a batch of tasks to be done before lunch. We'll talk more about batching and similar techniques in the next section of the book. This is specific to me as I work primarily as a developer, so your mileage may vary depending on your industry. Don't let me dissuade you though, if you're the type of person who wants to schedule very specific like this then by all means go for it!

Building Task Lists

When planning out my work I mentioned create a task list first, so I wanted to touch bit on having a task list. I build my task list in distinct ways.

The first is at the start of a project where I'll go through and create a massive task list. I'll simply jot down everything that comes to mind, and make sure it's recorded with all relevant information wherever I'm tracking my project. This can sometimes takes days if the project is long enough, and usually involves a lot of discovery and planning.

My other method is simply to add tasks as I think of them. Requirements changes, ideas come to mind, and so much else happens that can give me new ideas for tasks. Whenever these come to mind I makes sure to record them in my backlog. On that note, my backlog is simply a long list of tasks that I haven't yet scheduled. These are typically grouped by project and priority, but do what works for you.

Breaking Down Tasks

One thing I find immensely helpful in building my schedule is breaking down tasks. Attacking too big of a task is a good way to get discouraged and I've found myself procrastinating when I don't properly break down tasks.

My rule of thumb, is that if a task is estimated to take me an entire day or more then I need to break it down. Often I break down even smaller tasks just to make them more manageable.

I highly encourage everyone to break large or medium tasks into sub-tasks that are easier to digest. This makes it easier to both approach the task itself, as well as plan out how long it will take to complete. It's almost always easier to estimate a smaller task than a larger one.

Another benefit I find with breaking down tasks is the psychological boost you get when marking tasks complete. It can be encouraging to see a slew of completed tasks, and for many (including myself) it can be very motivating.

Kanban

I wanted to touch on Kanban quickly here as it's so important to way I, along with many others, work. Kanban is simply a way to organize tasks, and in the simplest implementations is a board with the column "TO-DO, "In Progress", and "Done". As you work, you move tasks across the board into their appropriate columns.

The benefit of this is that it provides a visual and tactile way to see where your tasks are. There are a lot of online software that includes Kanban boards, but a white board in your office is another popular way to build one. You can also add more columns to easily fit your workflow; for example I often add and "In Review" column between "In Progress" and "Done".

I typically add all the tasks for the week/month I talked about above into my Kanban board, and then use that to view my progress throughout the week. I highly recommend everyone give it a try. While there is a lot more to Kanban than just the concept of the board, I find it to the best most important for entrepreneurs to utilize.

Learning To Delegate

I wasn't 100% sure where the best place to put this part was, but since it ties in so closely with the 80/20 rule I feel like at the end of this chapter is fitting. Learning how to delegate tasks is a great way to build extra time into your schedule, and while it's certainly not for everyone I would be remiss if I didn't mention it here.

Now, I'm not going to go super in depth here as a complete guide on delegation deservers a book of its own. This will just be a nice primer on why you should start thinking about it, and how to start moving in that direction.

Delegation is one of the easiest ways to free up time, but it's not as easy as just sending off some working and calling it a day. Finding good people to work with, keeping them on track, and making sure their work is quality is a difficult process. I don't want to say that to turn you off, but just want you to keep in mind that it's not a free ride. When done correctly though, the benefits are enormous.

I also want to point out that this is not for every business at every stage. It takes some capital investment, no one works for free, and depending on the size of your businesses that might not be in the cards right now; and that's perfectly fine. Certain businesses might also benefit from it less, very in person companies might find what they can delegate limited outside of traditional employees.

It's also important to realize that they're multiple types of people you might find to delegate work to. For a more established business this usually takes the form of employees, either full or part time. For many small businesses the prospect of hiring an employee is far off; but luckily there are other ways to get people working for you. With the advent of the digital age, there are numerous ways to hire freelancers and contractors for small or ongoing projects.

Working with a freelancer on a contract basis is a fairly easy way to start delegating tasks. It can be a bit involved of a process, but suffice to say here it can be done cheaper and easier than hiring a full employee. This makes it a great place to start, especially when you don't have a set amount of hours to work each week. When done in this manner the delegation of tasks is often called outsourcing as you're moving the work out of house.

Getting Over The Superman Syndrome

Something many business owners suffer from, myself included, is what's lovingly called superman syndrome. This is the tendency for us to want to do everything, or have a hand in every decision. While this is fine at first, it quickly becomes impractical as your business grows.

I know how it feels, you've spent all this time working on your baby, it can be scary giving some control over to someone else. It's essential though as no one individual has the time or skills to do anything. Whether it's outsourcing, hiring your first employee, or taking critical criticism it's important to open up your business. It's the only way to grow past a certain point.

One of the first things I started outsourcing was design work. Being a developer, creating good designs was always my weak point; while they were serviceable they would take me forever and still not come close to a professional's quality. Recognizing this weakness was a big step, and finally starting to put that work on others not only made my end product better, but made me happier as I was free to focus on what I enjoyed doing.

What Tasks To Delegate?

Another big question is exactly what tasks should I be Delegating? The answer is generally try to get as much of that 80% of less important work off your plate as you can. That might be stuff like social media posts, create marketing graphics, and other things like that.

You also might want to consider outsourcing things you're not particularly skilled at, as a developer I often bring on help for a lot of my design work, and that helps me focus on what I'm actually good at and enjoy. There's no shame in hiring someone to help with something you're not good at. Most of us wouldn't try to fix electric problems on our own, we'd call an electrician. Your business is no different, just substitute electrician with another professional, unless your lights are out of course!

I always suggest people start with something that is not super important to their businesses or something they often forget to do. For example, maybe you want to post more to social media, but forget to block out time to come up with creative posts. This is the perfect thing to start with as it's small, and won't have a huge effect on your business.

It's also something that can be done cheaply and quickly. This both gives you an easy way to see the quality of the work the person does, as well as make your risk fairly low. In this way, it's best to start with small, cheap, and quick tasks as you get to know the person before you trust them to take on larger projects.

Once you do find good professionals though always make sure to keep in touch with them. Even if you don't need their service right now you never know when you will again. Cutting out the whole hiring process and having an expert to turn to right away is a huge time saver.

It can be a bit scary at first, but delegating or outsourcing is work for sustained business growth; there simply isn't enough hours in the day for one person to do everything.

Action Points

We've spent some time talking about planning and scheduling, and now it's time to put that information into action. I've put together the next couple action points to get you started on creating your own, and hopefully to help you become more efficient in your day to day work.

1. If Not Already Start Time Tracking

I'm going to mention it again here because if you're not it becomes very difficult to properly block time for tasks. Track your time, at least until you become pretty consistent in your estimates. You want to be able to look at a block of a couple hours and accurately guess which tasks will fit into it. You might already be pretty good at this, but I'd still recommend tracking for a time just to be sure you're on track with reality, as well as to potentially discover areas where you could be more efficient.

2. Figure Out How To Plan

By this I mean figure out how you want to record your planned tasks. Whether it's through a desktop program, a phone app, or just good old pen and paper, it doesn't really matter. What does matter is that you're comfortable with it and are committed to keeping it up to date. Then, stick with whatever you choose for at least a couple of weeks. So much time is wasted flopping between systems, resist the urge to do so.

3. Identify Important Tasks

If you don't know what's working it's hard to properly focus your efforts. That's why it's critical to identify your most important tasks and the one's that give you the best return on your time. This is also an ongoing process, not all tasks will maintain their importance forever, and many of them might be one-off and be replaced in the next week or month.

4. Sit Down and Plan the Next Month

While you might not stick with it, I'd would suggest starting by doing planning a month in advance. I like going by months as it's usually easy to break your yearly goals down into them. Having the goals in mind then makes it really easy to plan what you need to get done.

I find that first I like to brainstorm all the tasks I need to complete, then sort them into the weeks based on time and importance. If you're having trouble with planning, working backwards from your goals is the easiest way to keep you on track.

5. Check Back Often

Lastly, make sure you're checking your schedule often and making it a habit everyday. I personally start my day with my coffee by going over today's work and creating a plan of attack. The more you do this, the more it will become part of your routine. Getting into the routine can be difficult at first, but stick with it and it gets easier.

6. Consider What To Delegate/Outsource

I say consider outsourcing as not every business can or wants to, and it's certainly not a hard requirement. That said, if you can outsource, even a few hours of work a week, you'll free yourself up to focus on more important tasks. A good place to start is offloading a few hours to a virtual assistant or freelancer. This can be a quick and cheap way to get started, and poses little risk if things go awry.

Concentration and Procrastination

Two of the big killers, lack procrastination and lack of concentration have ruined many a night of work. I know I've had the days where I've done nothing but watch videos online, and I'm sure I don't have to tell you how unproductive those days were.

Conquering the urge to procrastinate and getting in the zone are two skills that all successful people have. In this section we're going to look at both of these, and talk about some techniques for making your working hours more effective. It doesn't matter how much time you spend scheduling if you never get any work done after.

As mentioned elsewhere in this book, none of these are silver bullets or applicable to every situation. Some of these are definitely going to be more effective and relevant to you than others. That's okay, everybody is different and I wanted to make sure to cover a wide range of techniques to help as many people as possible.

The best way to use these tips is to figure out where your concentration lacks and what causes you to procrastinate and then focus on techniques related to those. For example if you're a big video watcher what you can do to be more efficient is different than someone who is an email lover. Do what works for you, and then disregard the rest.

Figure Out Why You're Procrastinating

The first step to fixing any problem is to find the cause. This is a bit of self reflection, so sit down and be honest with yourself. Figuring out the root cause of what makes you procrastinate is key to figuring out what you can do to prevent it in the future.

If you've been tracking your working hours you might be able to find out the what and why. If unpleasant tasks seem to send you off then you know where to focus. If you see yourself spending too much time on social media, well then you have the answer to what.

It's also important to keep the past in the past. So you've procrastinated your whole life, who cares? Today is a new day and a chance to start new. Many people get caught up on their past failures and let it influence the present. Once a procrastinator does not mean always a procrastinator. Think positive thoughts, and seize the day with a renewed vigor!

Remove Distractions

One of the biggest causes, and consequently the first thing to look at, is the endless distractions that keep us from our work. This has gotten worse in the modern age with things like cellphones, Youtube, Facebook, and countless other distractions only a few seconds away.

Millions of hours are wasted each year by people getting distracted by this and others, so getting it under control is key to stopping procrastination. Removing distractions from your workspace is the easiest way to prevent them from influencing you.

To start, determine what types of distractions seep into your day. The common offenders are phone, social media, and email, but anything can be a distraction. This problem becomes twice as bad for those that work at home where even things like cleaning the house can be distracting. The only time I've enjoyed washing the counters was when I was putting off more important work.

Once you know what distracts you then you can take steps to remove it. For a lot of stuff, it's as easy as removing it from your workspace. I'll often leave my phone in the other room when I'm working so it doesn't distract me.

For websites there are certain browser tools which will block access to specific sites for a specified time. These are good options for those who just can't resist checking it during their work. I personally also make sure to close any browser tabs I'm not using for the work at hand to prevent any sort of distractions.

Setting boundaries is also another effective strategy that works for many. For example, you might say you have to compete 3 tasks before you can check Facebook, or limit social media to break times. Giving yourself these limits works almost like a reward system. For many, it helps them concentrate knowing there's a clear reward for doing so. Reward based working is a great way to keep yourself focused during working times.

As you work through this chapter, you'll find that many of these tips will help you improve your ability to concentrate and resist distractions. Keep this, as well as your own weaknesses, in mind as you read through the rest. Then, use the ones that apply to you for the best results.

Keep Your Important Tasks in Mind And Avoid Task Over-Load

The first tip is to simply keep the important things you have to get done at the front of your mind. A little bit of guilt for not working goes a long way to keeping you focused!

This is also why making the schedule earlier is so important. If you write your tasks down and have them to focus on it makes it so much easier to avoid distractions related to not knowing what to do.

In fact, one of my biggest problems in the past was what I call task-overload. I would have multiple projects going at once, and each one with a large number of tasks. I would sit and know I have all these tasks to do, but really not have a plan on what needed to be done and where I should start. So, instead of diving right in I would just kind of sit there and procrastinate, not really sure where to start.

This is a problem I and many have, and honestly a really easy to trap to fall into. Fortunately, if you've followed some of the steps earlier in this book you should have a schedule keeping you on track and have your important tasks fresh in your mind.

Having a good schedule also prevents procrastination due to not knowing where to start. There's been many times where I've been excited to jump into a big project, only to spend the next few hours half working because I really didn't have a plan where to start. Make a good schedule, and that won't happen again.

I also really encourage everyone to keep their schedule front and center. I personally take all my tasks for the day and put them onto a whiteboard in my office. This forces me to keep my tasks at the front of my mind, which in turn keeps me focused. I also really like the physical aspect of this as it lets me close my project management application which has the potential to be its own distraction.

Don't Over Prepare

Another big problem I've, along with many others, have had is over preparing and not actually starting work. There has to be a point where you jump in, even if things aren't a 100% clear yet.
Don't get me wrong, good prep is important, and I don't start anything without doing my due diligence. However, there is a point where you just have to start working, or you'd be sitting and preparing until the end of time.

This is a tricky one to gauge as preparation is a valuable task, and is necessary. It can be difficult to pick out the point where you've wandered into over prepared territory. Keep your mind on this, and when you feel like you're getting close it might be best to get to work and figure out the unknowns as you go.

This is similar to a trap a lot of perfectionists fall into. They may feel like they can't start a task until they do it perfect, or have a complete picture. This is unfortunately not how the real world works, and often times good enough is good enough. Getting something done is better than not doing anything just because it's not perfect. In most case, imperfect is just fine, and trying to achieve the idea of perfection is only serving to hold you back.

Being Busy Is Not The Same as Getting Work Done

A key point I want to touch on is just because your schedule is full that doesn't mean you're having a productive day. The saying goes work smarter not harder, and far too many people do the reverse.

There are a lot of us out there that fill our calendar and work hard, but a lot of the work isn't really doing what we need it to do. For example, maybe they're focused on unimportant tasks, and pushing the ones that will really drive growth off. This is a classic example of someone who is staying busy, but isn't really getting anything meaningful done.

This is part of the reason why in the scheduling section I talked so much about finding the important tasks. If you know what's important to your businesses you can spend your time focusing on that.

Someone who is busy but not productive might also be falling into some of the procrastination traps listed here. Maybe they spend all their time planning but not doing, or they spend weeks fixing minor issues of a project that no user will ever notice. While they're getting "work" done it doesn't really do much to get them closer to their goals.

Ask yourself whenever you're working if the work you're doing is part of your success. If it isn't, then you might be more busy than productive.

The One Minute Principal

Another small little trick I use in my day to day life is what I call the minute principal. In short, if something takes less than a minute to do just do it right now.

I'll find in a lot of cases I'll push small tasks off, and then either forget to do them or have them back up to the point where I'm spending an entire day addressing them. For example, I had a streak where I would write an article, and then put on my calendar to come back and do some of the very basic SEO work. I won't get into that here, but suffice to say this particular work only took about a minute to do. Crazily enough, it probably took more time to add it to my to-do list than to just do it.

For some reason though, I would push it off and not do it right away. Sure enough, a few weeks passed and now I had enough to do where it ate up several hours of my day and ruined my productivity for the day.

Now, I always take care of those small little tasks as they come up and just get them out of the way. It feels good to get stuff done, and it prevents them coming back to haunt you in the future. If it takes less than a minute just do it and have it off your mind for good.

Learn To Say No

A little secret of the very successful is that they love to say no. That may be a bit of a hyperbole, but the truth is that those who know how to manage their time also know how valuable it is. They don't just take any and every proposal that comes their way; they are able to properly evaluate it and decide where their time is best spent. Learning to say no is key to taking back your time.

This relates back to the principle of working on the most important tasks first. If something comes your way that isn't important, then it's okay to say no to it. Being the yes man is not the way to wrangle in your time.

These tasks could come from outside sources, or be ones that you think of throughout the day. Just because it's something you've come up with doesn't mean it's automatically important. Make sure you also learn to say no to yourself, and keep minor tasks off your plate or on a separate low priority list. Saying no to unimportant work is important to keep you on schedule.

Eliminate Half Work (Fully Focus On The Task at Hand)

Related to multi-tasking, one of the big problems with today's age is the amount of distractions available. It's easy to start a task, and then check your email, check your phone, look at some news ect. There's simply so much competing for our time it's difficult to know where we should focus. The fact is many of these might be important to your work, so it's impossible to just not do them. Trying to do multiple things at once though often leads to what's called half work, and that's no good either.

That's why when we work we should aim to focus on a single task at a time. We touched on that in multitasking myths easier, but it deserves to be said again here.

If you're going to be working make sure your focus is only on that. 5 hours of half working is time wasted. In order to get the most out of my work day I practice what's called task batching.

Task Batching

One of my favorite methods for getting stuff done is what's called task batching, although it can go by several other names. At its core though, the idea is to group like tasks together to increase productivity. In this section we'll take a look at that a bit more, and see why it's such an effective technique.

The big key with why task batching is so effective goes back to multi tasking, starting to see a pattern here? As was touched on earlier, our brains are not wired for multi-tasking. We are not good at switching tasks too quickly, and doing so requires mental effort to get us into the correct state to work on the new task.

This effort is only increased as the differences between tasks is increased. The more un-alike two tasks are, the more difficult it is to make that mental switch. That's not to say you can't do it, but it's certainly not the most efficient. This mental effort then leads to both less efficient work, and is a key spot where many people start to procrastinate. Task batching aims to stop both of those.

The key idea of task batching is that you take multiple like tasks, and then aim to work on them during the same block of time. I mentioned earlier that I like to batch my tasks, and this is exactly it.

For example, I might spend my AM hours doing programming, and then set the PM for writing. Both of these tasks are quite different, and batching them together helps me stay focused. I'm big on getting "In the zone" and once I'm in it no distraction can stop me. But, take me out and my productivity collapses. I know I'm not the only one that feels like this, and task batch helps me enormously.

Before I was task batching I would interweave my days with various tasks, and would find myself stopping and taking breaks as my brain tried to switch modes. If this is something you find yourself doing then you're like me, and task batching is going to help you out tremendously.

To put it into practice is quite simple, just aim to work on like tasks together. I like to split my day between morning and afternoon, but you can dedicate entire days to a single task type. For example, maybe I set Monday as programming and Tuesday as writing. The time periods you set aside don't really matter, the key is to simply not be switching between tasks too often.

You can also use task batching with other techniques as well. Take for example the idea of doing your most important task first. You can still do that with task batching, simply start your batch of tasks by doing the most important or least pleasant task first. Task batching is great because it so easily integrated with other techniques while being a super efficient way of getting work done.

Task batching is also great to help work across multiple projects. One of the most difficult things to do is work between different projects, and task batching has really helped me in this regard.

Many of my projects require writing for example, so on a writing day I'll be able to tackle each of them. I go a step further, and batch my batches by project. I'll take my AM batch, and then say each hour I'll work on a new project with a short break in between. This is what's so cool about task batching as it's very powerful, but super customizable to the individual.

Lastly, task batching lends itself quite well to the visual planners out there. It's very easy to assign each type of task a color for example, and code that into your planner. You might make all writing tasks blue, and then can see at a glance your blocks of writing. Not all of us plan the same way, so it's nice that this technique works across a range of preferences.

The Good Kind Of Peer Pressure

As kids we were all told that peer pressure is bad, but now we're old and wiser that's not always the case. A bit of peer pressure can be a good, especially when used constructively

Having someone there to keep you accountable for your goals is a huge motivator, and the fear of letting someone down is a great way to stay focused.

Many teams have daily standup where they talk about their tasks for the day, as well as any sort of blockers or issues. This is a great way to add some accountability to your work as now you've made a commitment to getting it done. The big problem here is as individual entrepreneurs it can be hard to replicate this.

The best move is to find a close friend family member that you can talk to. Tell them your goals, and ask them to keep you accountable. It can be a bit annoying to have them check in on you, but it really helps as now it's not jut you.

There are also online communities that host similar daily standup that can help keep you on track. Being part of these communities is great for business owners looking to connect and hold each other accountable. Just don't end up spending too much time there!

Lastly, if you have a business partners or even people you work with they can act in this manner as well. In fact, they might be the best choice since they work so closely with you. The closer they are to your work, the more honest with them you have to be as you can't fool them into thinking you've done more than you have!

Perfection is a Myth

Another big issue that held me back for quite a while was the need to be perfect. I would hold off on releasing things or spend far too much time on unimportant issues because it wasn't perfect yet. At the end of the day though, nothing is ever really perfect, and striving for that is just going to hold you back.

Now, I'm not saying you should release garbage or something you're not proud of. You don't want to put something out there that isn't quality. The key is to realize though that at some point there is diminishing returns on time spent working on something. There comes a point where you have to take the plunge and release something, even it's only 98%.

One of the key ideas in software develop is the MVP, or the Minimum Viable Product. The idea is that you figure out the key benefit of your product, and then release a product that satisfies that without too much extra. This allows you to quickly release a product, get user feedback, and determine if the idea is something worth moving forward with.

While this is a very software development idea I think it has some lessons that can be easily applied to other disciples. I think too many people spend far too much time making something perfect, and then neglect to ever release their product. When looking at your project as an MVP the key is to release early, get feedback, and improve. Things aren't suppose to be perfect, and that's okay.

I also really like the idea of using the minimum viable product to scale back and focus on what really matters. I'm sure we're all guilty of having these crazy grand ideas, and the more grand the idea the more intimidating the idea of getting started can be. That's why I like to focus on what the minimum is to get the product out the door. This not only helps you ship the product quicker, but also prevents that sort of work paralysis where there's too much to do to know where to start.

In the end though, it's just important to recognize when the perfectionist in us is preventing us from getting work done. Sometimes it's okay to put an imperfect product out into the world, and that last little bit isn't necessary to do right now.

Take Breaks

There's absolutely nothing wrong with taking a few breaks here and there. It can help you get refreshed, and give you a clear mind state to get back to working. In fact, studies have show that people who take several short breaks per day are actually more productive.

The idea is that no one is completely productive 100% of the day. There's no way to stay focused and working all day long without taking a break. By taking breaks at strategic times, you can come back feeling refreshed and ready to go.

The amount of time between breaks varies. Some people say working for 25-30 minutes for a short break (maybe 5 minutes) is good, while others prefer working for an hour with a longer break (about 15 minutes). What you do is up to you, and some people will work better with different work lengths and break times. Find out what works best for you and stick to it.

To get the most out of your break try to get them to line up with events where you'd normally want to take a break. Maybe have one line up with a time where you'd normally grab a snack. Or, perhaps have one after a long meeting to help you clear your mind.

If possible, getting up and going outside or for a walk is a great way to get refreshed. This is especially true if you sit all day long in an artificially lit room. Getting a bit of natural light and fresh air always helps me feel refreshed, even if it's only for a few minutes.

Are You The Meeting King?

I don't know about you, but I hate pointless meetings. Actually, if you're reading this book then you probably do too, and it's no wonder as most meetings are pointless and probably could have just been a quick email. You'll hear a lot about how famous business owners detest meetings, and only hold them when and for only as long as needed.

If you're the type of person who likes to schedule a lot of meetings take a good look at how important those meetings are, and how much work actually takes place during them. You might be surprised to learn how much time is actually wasted in them.

Many tech teams have adopted a work flow called SCRUM. Most of the details are not important here, but the key point here is that they have a daily standup meeting. I mentioned this earlier, but to recap, it's a short (less than 15 minutes) meeting at the beginning of the work day where each person goes over their work and any blockers.

This is an effective meeting as it gives each team member some interaction, builds a commitment, all without taking up too much time. I mention here as it's an example of what a good meeting can be, and should serve as inspiration for you. It also takes place at the beginning of the day so as not to interrupt anyone once they get to work. Not all meetings are bad, but make sure they server a purpose and don't drag on longer than needed.

3 Steps To Getting Into The Zone

Last up for this chapter, I want to end it with my 3 tips for getting in the zone. These are what I personally do that signal it's time to get to work, and help me focus the best.

1. Gather All I Need

The first step is to make sure I have everything I need to get to work for the next 1-2 hours. Generally, I'll take a quick look at my tasks, and get everything ready to go. I'll pull up the websites I need, grab a pen and some paper, and a nice glass of water. That's usually all I need, but if there is anything else I make sure I have it now. Nothing breaks my flow like having to pause mid-work and go grab something. It's always hard to get back into the flow after that.

2. Put Away My Phone/Close Un-needed tabs

I have a bad habit of checking my phone/email/Facebook, so I make sure all that's put away before I begin. For websites, I make sure all the browser tabs are closed, and everything I need is already open so there's little temptation to get distracted.

For my phone, I physically put it away from me so I'd have to get up to grab it. Being lazy, the act of walking across a room is usually enough to overcome my desire to check it. For most people this should be doable, and I promise you'll be way more productive when you're not checking your phone every 5 minutes.

3. Turn On Some lyric-less Music

I find putting on some music is really helpful to help me concentrate. It drowns out outside noise, and gives me something pleasant to listen to, which personally helps me focus.

One thing I've noticed, songs with lots of lyrics, especially ones I know, are actually a negative. I find myself distracted by the song and singing along or paying more attention to the song than my work. To that end, I try to listen to songs without much lyrical content to them. Depending on my mood it's usually dance music or classical. I also found songs in languages I don't understand work a well.

Music isn't for everyone, but I find it a great way to get focused and keep away outsides distractions. I put this here as even if music isn't your think something else might be and you should work to discover that.

Action Points

Now that we've reached the end it's time to take action. These points will aim to keep you focused, minimize distractions, and stop procrastinating. If these sound like you then take action and become more productive.

1. Determine What Type Of Procrastinator You Are

There may be a small percentage of us that don't procrastinate, but for the majority of us we do at least sometimes. The first step is to figure out why we procrastinate, and what form that takes; whether we watch videos or plan excessively, it all serves to detract from our work. Before you implement any of these tips make sure you've nailed down the why and what.

2. Create a Distraction Free Workspace

No matter what kind of procrastinator you are, making your workspace distraction free is going to be beneficial.
For most of us, that's going to be removing things like our phones or tablets, and closing any distracting browser tabs. Others might go further like closing out their email or moving

to a different room if they work from home.

3. Put Procrastination Tips Into Practice

What you do here largely depends on where you find the most benefit. This chapter has laid out a wide range of techniques, all of which are great but might work better for certain individuals. After you've read through the chapter make note of the tips that you feel would work best for you and put them into practice.

4. Re-evaluate Yourself

Always take some time out after a few weeks to re-evaluate yourself and make sure that you see progress. If you do, then great keep it up! If not, then maybe it's time to go back try something new. The goal with this chapter is to make your working time more productive, so if you're not achieving that it's time to reexamine what you're doing on a day to day basis.

Make It Routine & Building Habits

The last of the 5 steps is to start making the things talked about above into routine habits. Having good habits is a powerful asset and helps you run almost on autopilot throughout the day. In addition to making scheduling a habit, it's also a good idea to start looking at the tasks you do often, and start building them into good habits that can drive business results.

Good habits make working easy, as you don't have to take any thought to perform them. Bad habits on the other hand are a detriment to your working day, and can be big sources of wasted time. Being able to identify the habits you have, and fixing those that are bad is a key attribute of many successful people.

A good place to start is with your scheduling and planning.

Turning that into a habit is a great way to keep your on track. I've personally built into my routine a little time each morning to go over my schedule, and over time that's just a habit that I've developed. I no longer really think about, it sort of just happens automatically.

That's only the tip of the iceberg though. There are tons of different tasks that lend themselves well to habits, and having them can greatly increase your productivity, and help keep you on track with repeating tasks.

In this section we'll look at exactly what habits are, and how building your routine around them can be very effective. You'll also learn about how to build new good habits, and how to effectively unlearn bad ones. With these tips at your disposal you'll be able to use habits to help keep your productivity at peak levels. Let's jump right in.

What is a Habit?

Many people will be able to describe habits they have, and for the most part that's good enough. When writing this book though, I wanted to come up with a more formal definition of what defines a habit. After a bit of research, I came up with the following 3 points that experts use to describe a habit.

1. They Occur Regularly - For any anything to classified as a habit, it has to occur regularly and consistently. This is probably the key point most people associate with habits, but as you'll see it's only the first criteria. In many cases this will be everyday, but sometimes you might have things you only need to do every week or month. You can still create habits out of these, but they just take a bit longer.

2. They Are Cued By Your Environment - This is important, a habit is cued by something in your environment that sets off the action. You don't consciously make the decision, but are triggered by something external. We'll look at an example in just a minute.

3. They Happen Without Thought - True habits happen without you having to think about them. After being cued by your environment, you naturally take the next action. That's your habit.

To put them all together, let's take a look at a simple example. Each morning, when I wake up, I put a pot of coffee on and enjoy a cup. This is my one of my habits. First, it occurs regularly, almost everyday at around the same time.

Next, it's cued by my environment. Me waking up is the sign that I should put on a pot of coffee.

Last, I don't have to think about it. I've put on coffee so many mornings now that I naturally wake up and brew it. It's to the point where I almost feel weird not doing it. When I'm on vacation for example, I feel weird when I'm not making coffee in the morning.

This should hopefully give you a decent understanding of what habits are, albeit in a simple form, and alludes to why they are so powerful in our lives. Good habits are extremely powerful and can help immensely on work as we tend to take the action without having to think about it. Build good habits around work, and you'll just naturally tend to get to work and stay focused.

On the flip side though, they can life ruining. Drug addiction is often times built out of habits, and has the power to easily ruin a person's life and destroy them financially. I bring this up as a what can be used for terrible loss can also be used to great gain. It also highlights that not all habits are good, and in this chapter we'll look at how we can break some of those bad habits.

How Environment Plays a Role

One of the key points above is how environments trigger habits. This is usually a bit of a new idea for a lot of people outside of the psychology realm, so I wanted to touch a bit more on it here. The fact is your environment is a key factor in driving habits.

When talking about environment we can mean a slew of

different things. For example time could be considered a factor, or location, an action, your mental state, or the people around you. The idea is that these are outside influences that are pushing you to perform a specific action after experiencing them.

For example, maybe you always go to grab a snack a specific time of the day. This is a habit you've built on time. Or maybe, you stop at a specific donut shop whenever you're in that part of your town. This is an action where location is the external stimuli. Maybe you tend to procrastinate when faced with a difficult task, an example of how your metal state can influence you.

The important thing to realize is that these sorts of environmental factors are what trigger our habits and tell our body it's time to take some specific action. If you can recognize that, you can use that to your advantage to make building new habits easier. It also helps you recognize what might be the trigger for negative habits, which in turn can help you break them.

Let's take an example, say you want to start writing 500 words each day. On it's own that's a simple goal, and a SMART one at that as it has a clear success/failure and is bounded by time. You might start by saying you want to write these 500 words in the morning, so that you can have the rest of your day to work.

"In the morning" is a poor environmental trigger for a habit. What does that really mean? When you first wake up, after you've had breakfast? What you choose needs to be specific enough that it clearly happens and isn't some arbitrary concept. There needs to a specific trigger that you can use to cue the habit.

"I want to write 500 words a day, I will do this right after pouring my morning coffee and sitting down". Now, this is better as it has a clear and specific trigger. Sitting down for the day with the morning coffee is something very specific that you can use to trigger the habit. For me this is actually my exact cue to setup my schedule, I do it right after pouring my coffee.

This is the important take away, while using your environment to build habits is smart, whatever cues you use have to be specific enough to actually generate a response. The more specific the action, the stronger of a trigger it will be, and the easier to build a habit. If you're using something too generic it's very easy to get distracted, procrastinate, or just not take action.

The Science Of Rewards

Rewards are something that a lot of people think of when trying to build habits. They do work, but not in the way a lot of people think. The problem is, most people use rewards as a way to build their habit, and lean on it too heavily. They also tend to give themselves too big of rewards, which is also an issue.

The big problem with using rewards to build your habits is that they then become the key motivator for the habit. If later you take the reward away, the desire to complete the action of the habit goes with it. A good reward isn't an incentive to do the task, but something that reinforces it.

The idea of a reward also takes out the key idea that a habit should require almost no thought. By introducing an element of consideration into the equation you make the habit less automatic and more of just a daily task.

That's not to say that rewards are bad, it's just that they need to be done right. With that in mind, let's look at what makes a good reward, and how you can reward yourself in a smart way.

Why Rewards?

The first important thing to understand is why rewards at all in the first place. I guess that's pretty easy to see, but we'll just touch on it briefly here.

Rewards overall give us a positive reason to do things. In most cases, we use the promise of a reward to keep us motivated. This is especially the case for long or difficult task.

With habits, they work much the same way, giving us encouragement to push through and complete the action.

However, unlike traditional tasks we want everything to be automatic, so we don't want to sit and think about what our reward is, it should just happen.

Rewards Should Be Related To The Habit

A good reward is something that is related to the habit or takes you deeper into it. Note, that doesn't mean that they are intrinsically related, just that the actions pair well together.

Let's go back and look at the writing example from earlier. You've decided that you'll write 500 words first thing in the morning, and your cue will be sitting down with your coffee. As a reward, after you're done you'll catch up on the news for a few minutes This might seem a bit strange at first, but let's take a look at it.

Firstly, the reward comes immediately after the habit. This is important as it helps to build positive reinforcement to task. Similar to how you rewards a dog right after it does something good, your reward should come right after completing the habit. This way you learn to associate the two together.

Second, the reward is related to the task. Not related in that they are both writing, but that they you've decided the news is an effect of finishing your writing. Do that enough, and you'll start to associate the two together creating that relationship for yourself.

Lastly, it's a small thing. The reward is not something large that drives you, but almost and afterthought of completion. This is key as too often the reward is far too large for the tasks, and becomes the sole motivation. In this case, the news is a nice bonus, but isn't the sole thing driving the habit.

In this way, we've created a reward that fits the problem space. We've also created one that doesn't take much thought and happens automatically lending well to the properties of a habit.

Improve The Enjoyability

The other type of reward that often works is something that directly impacts the enjoyability of your task. These are usually a big bigger and a one time thing, so I usually only use them after a long period of time for extended motivation.

Once again, going back to the writing example, you might buy a book that improves your writing skills. This is a good way to both reward yourself, as well as help make the activity more fun day to day.

Careful with this type of reward though, as it often is more likely to become your sole source of motivation. If you buy a new book every few weeks, what happens when you run out of books to buy? With the lack of incentive your motivation disappears and you lose the habit.

How Long Do Habits Take To Form?

How long a habit takes to form is a deceptively difficult question. You'll typically hear the two numbers 21 days and 66 days. Both have some merit to them, but it's not as clear cut as that.

The truth, is that everyone is different, and therefore everyone will build new habits at different rates. For some that might be very quick, while others will take longer before an activity becomes a true habit.

My go to has always been 30 days. There's no science behind it, I just think 30 days, or a month, is a nice, easy number to keep in mind. It's also not too short of time, so it ensures you'll spend a decent amount of time working on your new habits. I suggest setting 30 days as your goal, and then move the up or down depending on how that feels to you.

If 30 days seems a bit short, then 60 is another nice round number I like. Two months is a good amount of time. Performing something everyday for that span is a sure way to build a new habit.

We also briefly touched on weekly or monthly habits, and these take even longer to form. If the 30-60 days is based on doing it every day then you're looking at 30-60 weeks/months to nail down a longer running habit. This is a long time, and why these types of habits are difficult to create.

5 Steps To Creating New Habits

Now that we have a decent understanding of habits let's look at actually building one. Going back to my numbered lists, I've tried to condense the process down to 5 steps. These are the key ideas to building a new habit.

1. Choose Something Measurable and Specific

Much like goals, it's easier to build habits that are specific and measurable. "Get more done" seems nice, but it's impossible to really track, and is not something that you can specifically measure. This makes it a poor choice to a new habit as there really isn't anything concrete about it.

Being specific is also important as it's easier to focus on a specific task than a general one. Writing more each day is far too general, and it's difficult to know what that means. What constitutes more? Going with specific numbers, 500 words each day, makes the habit easier to form and easier to see progress.

Find something concrete and quantifiable, and stay away from ambiguous statements that have no clear end.

2. Start Small

It's easier to improve an existing habit than build a new one. Many people try to build new habits by jumping in at the deep end; I'm going to write 5000 words each and everyday. While having lofty goals is great, it's much easier to build a habit that is smaller and then add to it.

One of the key components of building a habit is repetition, and the lower the barrier to doing whatever task you've picked the more likely you are to follow through. If you try to write 5000 words a day you'll likely find it hard to actually hit that mark and might end up procrastinating and putting it off. This is the exact type of behavior building habits is trying to prevent! If you instead start with only 500 then you'll have a much easier time of sticking to it.

Sticking to it is really key, so make sure you pick something easy enough that you can easily complete it for the next 30-60 days without fail. Once you've done that, the task will become habit, and adding on to it will be easier. It's easier to go from 500 to 1000 words than the initial 500 words was, even though it's roughly the same amount of work.

3. Don't Try To Do Too Much At Once

It's always easier to focus on one thing over many, and building habits is no exception. If you're focused on one habit, you'll be more successful than trying to do 5 at once.

This goes back to starting small, it's easier to work in small chunks. While the habits themselves might be small, if you load too many on you'll end up with the same problem.

The common advice is to stick to building 1-2 small habits at once, and not try to tack on too many. This is a bit up to the person as some people are much better at pushing themselves than others. Keep in mind though, your goal is to do these things each day, and the more you take on the more you're going to have to sacrifice.

4. Recognize What You're Giving Up

Everything we do has an opportunity cost, the loss of taking the next best thing. When you're looking to build a new habit you usually have to give up something, there are only so many hours in a day after all.

Depending on your schedule, this could be something as minor as cutting out some tv or some internet browsing. In cases like this it's usually pretty easy to see what the better option is. You just need the willpower to choose the more productive option.

For others though, the choice might be harder. You might have to cut out some other work, or spend less time on certain tasks. This goes back to prioritizing as you need to understand which is better for your goals, the habit you're trying to build or the work it's replacing.

In any case, understanding what you lose is important as it can help you keep focused on building the new habit. If, for example, you give up television you can catch yourself if you start watching. You can use this as an easy check to make sure you're following through on your habit building goals.

5. Force Yourself To Do It Everyday

There's no way around it, if you want to build your new habit you'll need to do it everyday. It might be hard at first, but that's the kind of the point here.

You need to be on your game and force yourself to take whatever action it is each and every day, on time with your cue. This is extremely important for the first few weeks as this is the time when you set the foundation for your new habit. Even missing one day early on can mess up the whole process and force you to start over.

Many people try to build habits by half following them here and there, and then missing a few days in between. This type of half working doesn't work, and all you'll end up with is a task you do a couple days here and there.

There really is no secret here, if you followed all the other advice you have all you need to be successful. The rest falls on you to push through and stay committed.

It's not easy, but focus on the end result. Keeping your goals in mind is a great way to stay motivated. If you work hard, before you know you'll be doing your new habit without even thinking about it!

Breaking Bad Ones

We've talked a bit about building new habits, but what if you want to break a bad one? The idea here is very similar, but in reverse. Breaking a bad habit is similar to creating a new one, and requires a clear idea, the willingness to change, and persistence to work at it every day.

1. Recognize You Have a Bad Habit and Why

The obligatory first step is to recognize you have a bad habit. You can't do anything if you don't acknowledge it's there. You have to be honest with yourself here, and admit the problem upfront.

It's also important to understand why you have the habit. In a lot of cases it's the end result of the habit that makes it so appealing. Maybe you browse social media when you get stuck on a difficult problem, and this gives you a sense of peace during a difficult time. It's easy to see there that the social media is simply a conduit for the end result, and the bad habit is pushing off difficult work.

This is important to understand as you don't want to simply replace a bad habit with another for the end result. In the example above, maybe going to grab a snack is used to replace the social media browsing. This changes what the action is, but not in a meaningful way. The habit of pushing off the difficult work is still there and not any better.

Understanding the what and why gives you the power to fix both at once. Otherwise, you run the risk of simply changing the action without fixing the end result.

2. Determine The Cue

Closely related to the above, you also have to understand what triggers the bad habit. In the example above, it's getting stuck on a difficult problem that cues the action.

In most cases, there really isn't a fix for this as the cue is going to be something you can't change. There's no way to prevent difficult problems from occurring, you just have to live with them.

What you can do though, is recognize the cue, and use that to help you avoid the action. If you can see you've encountered a difficult problem, you'll be able to consciously know not to follow the bad habit. This self awareness is key in breaking the habit.

That's really the key to why habits are so powerful, you often don't even think about them, you just do them. That's why it takes so much effort to stop a bad one, you have to think and catch yourself before you do them. Recognizing what triggers the action of the habit is the next step in doing that.

3. Catch Yourself Doing It

Understanding all the things leading up to it is important, but you also need to be able to catch yourself during it. Once you can do this, it just takes a bit of willpower to stop and do something more productive.

This is the hardest part, and what is going to take the longest to master. It's an ongoing process, and it's okay at first if you don't completely knock it out. In many cases, you'll realize after the fact "Oh shoot I did it again". This is all part of the process, and gets better the more you work at it. Just keep it in your mind, and eventually you'll start catching it earlier and earlier.

4. Fill It With Something Else

The easiest way to stop doing something is simply to start doing something else. In a lot of cases, replacing a bad habit with a good one is the way to go.

What this looks like is up to you, and could be anything from taking a short break to just continuing what you were doing.

Maybe instead of browsing social media when you encounter a difficult problem, you simply just get back to work. It doesn't always have to be something new that you do.

You can also do this in steps. Take the above social media browsing for example. Let's just say that on average, you spend 15 minutes browsing it each time you let it distract you. Your goal is to completely stop taking these breaks, but you decide instead to replace it with 5 minutes away from your desk to start. By doing it in steps you make it easier, while reaping the benefits of that saved time quicker.

Action Items

We've come to the end of the habits section, and hopefully know you have an understanding of why they are so important. Good habits keep us subconsciously focused, and make work happen almost on auto pilot. I put this section here as once you make time planning and scheduling into a habit it becomes so much easier to do, but the lessons can be applied to all parts of your business.

1. Think Of a New Habit and Start Building It

This is a good time to start putting what you learned into practice, especially since it's fresh in your mind. Come up with one thing you want to turn into a habit over the next few months and get started with it.

If you're having trouble here look at the goals you set and find something that works towards that. Whatever it is, you should be moving towards your goals and improving your business. If you're really at a loss, making the process of planning and scheduling your new habit.

2. Time To Break a Bad Habit

If you've got a bad habit, and we all do, now is also a good time to start breaking it. Put in to practice the tips in this chapter, and use this as an opportunity to better yourself.

If you want, you can also segment step 1 and 2 out to run back to back. We talked about starting small, so there's no shame in picking 1 thing and working at it and then doing the other. Examine yourself, and look at what is going to increase your productivity the most, building a new habit or getting rid of a bad one.

3. Never Stop Improving

This is all an ongoing process, and you'll always have something more you can work on. Never stop looking for new ways to better yourself and become more productive in your business.

There's More To Effective Time Management

I know at the beginning of this book I talked about the 5 key points of time management, and we've gotten through all five. However, there's a bit more to it than that, and so I've included a few extra sections for those looking for a little bit more meat. Now, the 5 steps above are in my belief the most effective, and will give you a great place to start from, but there's no harm in learning more. These extra steps are just that, extras that can help you become a more effective business owner. Let's jump right in to the first section.

Master Your Inbox

One of the most crucial pieces of communication today is the email. While it certainly makes communicating easier, it also has the downside of potentially eating up hours of your day.

Learning to master your inbox is a key step to taking back many hours of your day. I know so many business owners who are swamped going through their emails that they find it eats up a ton of their time. Others have found themselves looking through their email as a distraction from their work; instead of a productivity tool it becomes one for procrastination.

If either of those sound like you, then this chapter is for you. Even if it's not, there might be some gems in here to help you save some time in your daily routine. I've added this chapter here as I know email is one of the biggest wasters of time for business owners, and it would be a disservice to you dear reader if I didn't include it.

To help you manage your inbox, I've compiled the top 8

strategies that I use to help keep my inbox in good shape. Each one of these is something I've done, or continue to do each day to help keep my inbox clean and me focused on actual work.

Create a Dedicated Time

The first step to wrangling in lost time spent on your inbox is to stop checking it constantly. I've fallen into this trap before, where I'll have my email open and constantly be checking for new emails.

We talked a bit earlier in this book how multitasking doesn't work, and this is a prime example of it. Every time you stop working to check your email your brain needs to make that switch to the new task. This makes it harder to get back into what you were doing, and your focus will suffer because of it.

Instead of looking at it all day, setup periodic times to go through and address the new emails. I like to do this at beginning of the day, at lunch, before I leave, and once more throughout the day. That ends up being roughly every 2 hours

I spend a couple of minutes going through my emails.

This method is way more effective, and doesn't take me out of the flow of my work. I'm able to go through and mark all of my emails, and then get back to focusing on my work until the I do the next batch later.

With this method it takes a little extra time to go through all the emails, but ultimately saves more as I'm not wasting time checking every few minutes. It also increase my productivity as now I'm more focused on the task at hand, and not on emails that are coming in.

Take Action Immediately

The next step is to not fall into the trap of letting emails sit; when you read one decide what to do with it. This helps reduce clutter, and prevents you from wasting time on an email you've already read.

This tip helps you make sure your inbox is always clean, and that everything important is addressed. I'll often times read an email, think "maybe I'll get to it later", leave it there and have it clog up my inbox for a few days before I take action.

This is not an efficient way to do things as now you're having to read and process the same mail twice, and sometimes even more than that. Instead, knock it out right away. For the majority of emails this means either replying to the email, or simply deleting it. By making sure to do this on every email every time you check it you'll reduce all the noise and save yourself time later.

For those that truly can't be done now, use labels and folder to organize them. We'll take a look at that in the next step.

Use Labels and Folders

For emails you want to save or process later setting up labels or folders is a great way to do so. Most email clients allow your to set up folders or other tags so you can sort or categorize your emails.

This is also a good way to save emails for later without them hogging up your main inbox. Perhaps there's some important details in an email you might want to reference later. Simply create a folder for important mail, and move it there to clear out your inbox.

In most programs you can create as many folders as you want so it's easy to get as specific as you like. You could for example segment important emails by sender, or create folders for emails related to specific projects. Find out what works for you, and strike a balance between too many and too little.

Some email clients even let you split your inbox and automatically sort incoming mail by various criteria. You might for example sort email from within your company and those from external sources. Gmail for example is able to determine things like updates, promotions, and things of that nature and sort them automatically for you. Leveraging features like this can save you a lot of time having to set it up on your own.

Unsubscribe From Un-needed lists

It seems like every website has a mailing list these days, and if you're like me you've probably signed up to a few of them. While a few that provide good content is great, it's easy to go overboard and end up with tons of un-needed subscriptions.

The next time you're going through your email take note of all the subscription emails you get. How many do you actually read? It's probably way less than the number you're subscribed to.

If you see one that you don't read, then cancel the subscription. You can always come back a re-subscribe if you made a mistake, but odds are you won't. This serves to clean up your inbox, saving you time in the long run. It's a simple step, but will pay back tenfold.

Use a personal email

One thing I do to help keep work and life separate is to have a different personal email. This is what I use for things like the above mentioned newsletters, as well as for signups for personal sites.

This separation greatly cuts down on the amount of emails I have to process during the workday. My work email then gets no sort of mail related to newsletters, shipping from Amazon, or notifications from social media. This saves me a lot of time overall.

I also then don't feel as obligated to keep up with my personal email. Since everything in there is relatively unimportant I can let it grow or set up automatic deletion rules after a certain amount of time has past.

Use Other Methods of Communication

Not really an inbox trick, but sometimes email is overused. There are times where instant messaging, phone call, or a simple walk over to the other person is much more productive.

This not only more effective in most cases, but saves room in your inbox. A 5 minute talk is often better than an entires day worth of back and forth over email.

Never neglect other communication channels. Just because you can email doesn't mean you always should.

Reply Selectively

Not every email warrants a response. Remember, it's always easier to just delete an email than come up with a response for it. While it won't work for every email, many actually do need a response, don't reply just for the sake of replying.

I'm a big fan of not saying something if you have nothing to say. That's why I hate getting emails like "Okay", or other very simple replies that really don't add any value. I can understand the need to confirm in some cases, but in others it's unnecessary.

Don't feel like you need to respond to every single email. It's okay to just quietly delete some emails, and save you the time of composing a reply.

If you really must reply some email clients give the ability to regenerate short messages like "Thanks", or "Sounds Good". These can save time constantly typing out the same response while showing the sender you did read their message.

Consider Templates

Last up, if you send a lot of emails of the same type consider creating a template that you can re-use. This saves you a ton of time in having to write an email, as well as having to re-figure out the wording each time you write it.
If you're in this boat this is a huge time saver. For example, you might be a business that provides some type of service, and whenever a potential client contacts you they receive the same email. This is a perfect candidate for creating a template.

A photographer might have a standard email that they send out with a list of their services and prices. For an in demand photographer they might send this out multiple times per day. By creating a template for it, they can much more quickly send it out, and spend less time managing their email.

Get creative here. Once you see yourself sending the same email a few times it might be a good idea to create a simple template so you no longer have to write it each time. A few minutes per week over the course of a year is a good amount of time saved.

Action Items

With the above tips in mind it's time to wrangle in your email. This section is kind of light, just like your email should be! While all the tips above are good, the only one that is universally applicable is to set aside a dedicated email time. This can be once a day, or multiple times depending on your workload. The goal is to make this the only time you check your email, and not get distracted and bogged down on it the rest of the day. The rest of the tips are great, and make sure to use them as you see fit, but this is by far the most important.

Working From Home Tips

I debated whether to put this chapter in, but I thought it would be a good idea for a book about making the most of your time. Many business owners spend at least a portion of their time working from home, and many employees are given the option too. With that it's important to know how to do so effectively and make the most of your time in a typically non-productive environment. I know this chapter won't apply to everyone, but for those that it does hopefully it can help you be more productive.

The problem with working from home is how difficult it can be to be productive. Your home is a place where you often relax and enjoy your time, so it can be tricky to get yourself to see it as a working zone. Rife with distractions, the home is usually not the most ideal place to work. Like all things though, there are some tricks to making it just as effective as your office, and much more convenient to boot.

The following are the tricks I've come up and put into practice to help me be just as productive at home as I am in the office.

Create a Dedicated Workspace

The fist step I give to anyone working from home is to setup a dedicated space to work. Lounging around on the couch might seem nice, but I can guarantee you won't be productive doing that. Having a set place to go to work is key to getting in the right head space, and seriously helps to avoid getting distracted.

Being too comfortable leads to lack of production and increases the odds you'll procrastinate, at least it does for me. That's why I never work on the couch or in bed. I simply can't focus enough to get anything done. I'm going to go out on a limb and guess that's true for most people.

If you have the space, setting up a separate office is the best move. This gives you your own segmented space to keep all your work materials, and provides the best separation of work and home. It's also a great way to signal you're in working mode. This is especially important if you have roommates or family that live with you and they tend to disturb you. Set some boundaries on not to interrupt you when you're in your office, and prevent all those little distractions.

For those that don't have an office space, then setting up a small desk, or even a folding table, in the corner of a room is another great option. It doesn't need to be fancy, just a place where you can sit down and get to work and not be distracted. The further away from the "fun stuff" in your home the better. Something like a guest bedroom, or other out of the way area is perfect. Less ideal are areas like a living room where you might have a television and easy access to other distractions, but they will still work in a pinch.

The idea is to create an area of your home that signals it's time to get to work. This is very important when you work from home as you're often in an environment that you associate with relaxing and play. You don't have the clear indicator like going into the office has, so make sure to take some time and do this for yourself. It also gives you a nice separation between home and work which we'll touch on a bit at the end of this chapter.

Double The Importance Of Distraction Removal

This is a huge point, and twice as important as when working outside the home. While at work we have our phones and the internet to distract us, at home we have even more like TV's, video games, and whatever else you keep in your home. I even spent time happily cleaning over getting to work before, so even "chores" can end up being distractions. Never in my life has I even considered vacuuming at the office, but when working from home it seemed like a great idea.

When you're setting up your workspace as detailed earlier, make sure to choose an area that is distraction free, or at least remove the distractions while you're working. If you have the option, work in a space bedroom with no TV over the living room that has your entertainment system. If it's possible to move some of these distractions away while you work then do it. You'll thank yourself later when you're actually getting stuff done and not watching the news again.

The further you can remove yourself from any distractions the better. We touched on this a lot in the procrastination section, and it's only more important here. The more temptations there are the harder it is to resist, and there is no place with more temptations than your own home. Make the smart move and remove them from your workspace.

Stick To a Schedule

Even though you're working from home, it's still a good idea to figure out a work schedule and stick to it. It's way easier to get to work once you have a routine down, one that you can follow each day and don't have to think about.

As an example, some people like to get up and still get dressed as if they were going to work. This helps get them in the work mindset, and if it's something that works for you then go for it.

Small things like this signal it's time to work, and really help some people get and stay focused.

This also includes things like taking breaks or lunch at designated times. Don't fall into the trap of taking trips to the kitchen every 5 minutes to grab a snack. This is just another form of procrastination, and is going to add up over the week. 5 minutes here and there quickly quickly turns to an hour or two of missed work.

My recommendation is to find a schedule that works for you and stick to it. Wake up, shower, grab some coffee, and get to work; that's mine. I follow a very similar flow each day to start, and it helps get me awake and ready to work. Find out what works for, and then stick to it.

Stay Connected

One of the biggest drags of working from home is the lack of human interaction, but it doesn't have to be that way! With the huge variety of chat programs out there, it's easy to stay connected, and can help keep you motivated during the long, lonely work day.

If you're part of a team, keep your chat program open and touch base with your colleagues throughout the day. Do take care though to not let it become a distraction.

Even if you're not part of a team, having a chat program to talk to your friends, business associates, or fellow entrepreneurs is a good way to keep in contact and keep your sanity.

That's one of the things they don't say about working from home is how lonely it can be at times. This in itself can end up demotivating you and hampering your work output. Take a bit of time to engage with some other humans from time to time, especially if you're a naturally social person.

You also have the option to get out every once in a while. I personally spend some time working at local coffee shops a few times a month just to get out of the house and get a change of scenery. It's also nice as there are less distractions there than in my home.

When You're Done You're Done

Another big problem I've noticed many entrepreneurs have is no semblance of work life balance. Since they work from home, they're never really out of the office, and end up working crazy hours or taking emails at 3am.

While this is fine on occasion, you do need some sort of work/life balance or you risk burning yourself out. Very few people can successfully work 60+ hours a week for months on end without burning out and loosing huge amounts of productivity. It's also pretty poor for your health to push yourself that much for that long.

That's why I always suggest spending your evenings away from your work, and take some time for yourself. Having a dedicated workspace as mentioned above makes this easy, as once you leave that the work day is over. It's okay to take breaks from your work, and is usually more productive to do so in the long run than killing yourself with crazy hours and burning out.

Watch Your Health

Lastly, it's important to watch your health. Many of us are rabid in our dedication to our work, but we shouldn't let that impact the quality of our life.

This is an easy pit to fall into for work from homers as it's easy to stay locked in all day working. With no pressing need to leave the house, it's easy to let the hours slip by locked in your office. I know I've gone days without going outside or doing any appreciable exercise, and that's not a good thing.

There's a lot that goes into health and fitness, and I'm not going to get into here as that's outside the scope of this book. Suffice to say, it's important.

Getting a bit of exercise and eating right go a long way to staying healthy. It's also been shown to help improve focus, and improve productivity in the long run. Don't neglect your health just to get a few hours of extra work in, it's not worth it.

Oh, and drink a lot of water, staying hydrated is important too!

Action Points

A shorter section, but one that I feel is going to be quite beneficial for most business owners who work from home. The key ideas here are that it can be difficult to stay focused while working from home, but not impossible.

1. Create a Dedicated Workspace

My first suggestion is always to create dedicated workspace. It doesn't have to be fancy, just a space in your home where you can go to signal it's time to work. Everything from a home office, to a folding table in a corner of a room work perfectly fine.

2. Find a Schedule

Even though you're at home, sticking to a schedule is important to stay productive. This can include everything you might normally do on your way to work, or simply just be roll out of bed and get to work. The content isn't important, it's the consistency that is key.

3. Don't Overwork

Lastly, take some time for yourself and don't burn yourself out. Work/life balance can be hard to achieve when working from home, so take steps to build that separation. Also, watch your health and make sure you're taking proper care of yourself and getting out frequently. A healthy body is a more efficient body in all things it does.

My 10 Killer Productivity Tips

This last section I wanted to make a sort of cheat sheet that you can look back to. I wanted to provide some type section where if this was all you read you would still be able to derive some benefit from this book. Think of it like the spark notes version, all the goods of this book condensed as best I could.

I also wanted it to be a nice point of reference for those who actually read the whole book. This is a good place to look back to and get fresh ideas about the key points of the book. I'll repeat myself a bit here, but that's on purpose because this is all so important.

1. Make a Written Plan

I can't stress this enough, but make a schedule and write it down. By writing I don't mean you have to use pen and paper, just anyway that gets it out of your head and into the world. Countless studies have shown that you're more likely to do stuff that you write down. It also just makes it easier to follow through on things as you can't just forget about them. This is great for both keeping you honest, as well as keeping track of how well you're doing and visualizing your progress.

2. Set SMART Goals

Smart is an acronym detailed earlier in this book, and the goals you set should follow it. This is a specific way of setting goals that makes sure the goals you're setting are trackable and have a deadline. Open ended goals don't work.

Having goals is super important as I've said several times throughout this book. Without goals there's no clear end point to be working towards, and that makes everything from planning to staying focused more difficult.

3. Track Your Time

If you're not by now, start tracking your time. It's essential to creating good schedules. It also helps you find areas where you might be wasting time.

It doesn't have to be fancy, but be honest. Don't keep the timer running if you spend the last half hour watching videos.

4. Work In Batches

I talked about batching in the procrastination section, and I truly believe it is one of the best ways to stay focused. By batching, you take like tasks and group them together. Very simple.

The idea is that you don't switch tasks as often, and therefore waste less time. Switching tasks is not free, and every time you do it your brain needs to adjust. This leads to loss of productivity and focus. By batching, you do this switching as little as possible.

5. Make Task Priorities

Making priorities is the best way to know what to do and when. With some many items competing for our attention, being able to rank tasks in order of importance makes planning much easier. This is also why setting goals is so important as you can map your tasks to them to help determine their importance.

6. Remove Distractions

One of the best ways to get in the zone is to remove distractions. If that's the only thing that you take away from the procrastination chapter this should be it.

Things like your phone, email, social media, tv, and so much more serve to distract us everyday. If you want to be as productive as possible then do your best to get them out of your workspace.

7. Kill Procrastination

When removing distractions isn't enough, spend a bit more time examining your habits. It's an eye opening experience to see just how much time you waste in a week.

There are lot of techniques for staying focused, but a lot of it depends on the individual. Once you learn why and how you procrastinate you can start using strategies to beat it.

8. Build Better Habits

Building good habits is an important step to working more effectively. Building habits takes time, but is well worth the effort.

It's also important to examine your bad habits and work on breaking them. Try to replace bad habits with good ones for twice the gain.

To start, try to make planning and scheduling your new habit. This is a great way to get organized and stay focused for years to come.

9. Conquer Your Email

So much time is wasted looking over emails, if you can cut

down on that you can save hours a week. Work on both organization as well as batching your email time to prevent wasting your hours on it.

10. Delegate

Lastly, if you're in the position start looking to delegate. Even hiring a freelancer for a few hours a week is enough to give you, well a few hours extra a week. The more you can delegate the more time you get back. It's difficult, but is key to keep a growing company growing!

Your Turn

We've come a long way, and I think we're better for it, at least I hope we are. Throughout this book we've talked a lot about scheduling, planning, and productivity, and I hope you can come away from it having learned something. Even If reading this only saves you a couple minutes each day, that will add up over time.

The last thing I want to leave you with is a call to action; take some action today while it's fresh in your mind. The only person holding you back is you. I know, that sounds like a bad motivational speech, but it's true. All the words in this book will do you no good if you don't put them into action and do something about it. So get out there, and start building something incredible!

Spare a Minute?

I'd like to thank you for reaching the end of this book. If you liked it, I'd really appreciate if you could drop a review on Amazon about it. If you didn't like it, then I think you bought this book somewhere else… But seriously, liked it, hated it, or somewhere in between let me know. My goal is to provide the best content I can, so I'm always looking for feedback, good or bad. I really appreciate it!

www.ingramcontent.com/pod-product-compliance
Lightning Source LLC
Chambersburg PA
CBHW021819170526
45157CB00007B/2648